This book is especially for

From

Given on

This book is dedicated to Fr. Andrew Mbiko, a visionary leader and a tireless advocate for Tuuru Water Scheme in Meru County. It is also a tribute to community water supply volunteers in Nyambene and around the world. NMM.
Additional books can be ordered from local bookstores and online booksellers.

Clean Water Comes to Karui's Home

Nkuchia M. M'ikanatha / Illustrated by Thelma Davis

Book design by Davia C. Lilly-Barnes

Water for the Village Press— Hummelstown, Pennsylvania

Karimi, Karui and Marete

For Isaac Batian and all the other curious children interested in stories about people in villages far from their homes—with admiration, NMM & TID.

Nkuchia M'ikanatha, DrPH, MPH and Thelma I. Davis, Ed. D. assert the right to be identified as the author and illustrator of this work.

Library of Congress Control Number: 2009902598.

ISBN: 978-0-578-52032-2

EAN: 9781439232934

At sunrise, while her family is sleeping,
Karimi leaves her home on the long walk to fetch water.

On the road to the spring,
Karimi is joined by her friend Kaedo.
They walk with many others who are going
to get water for their families.

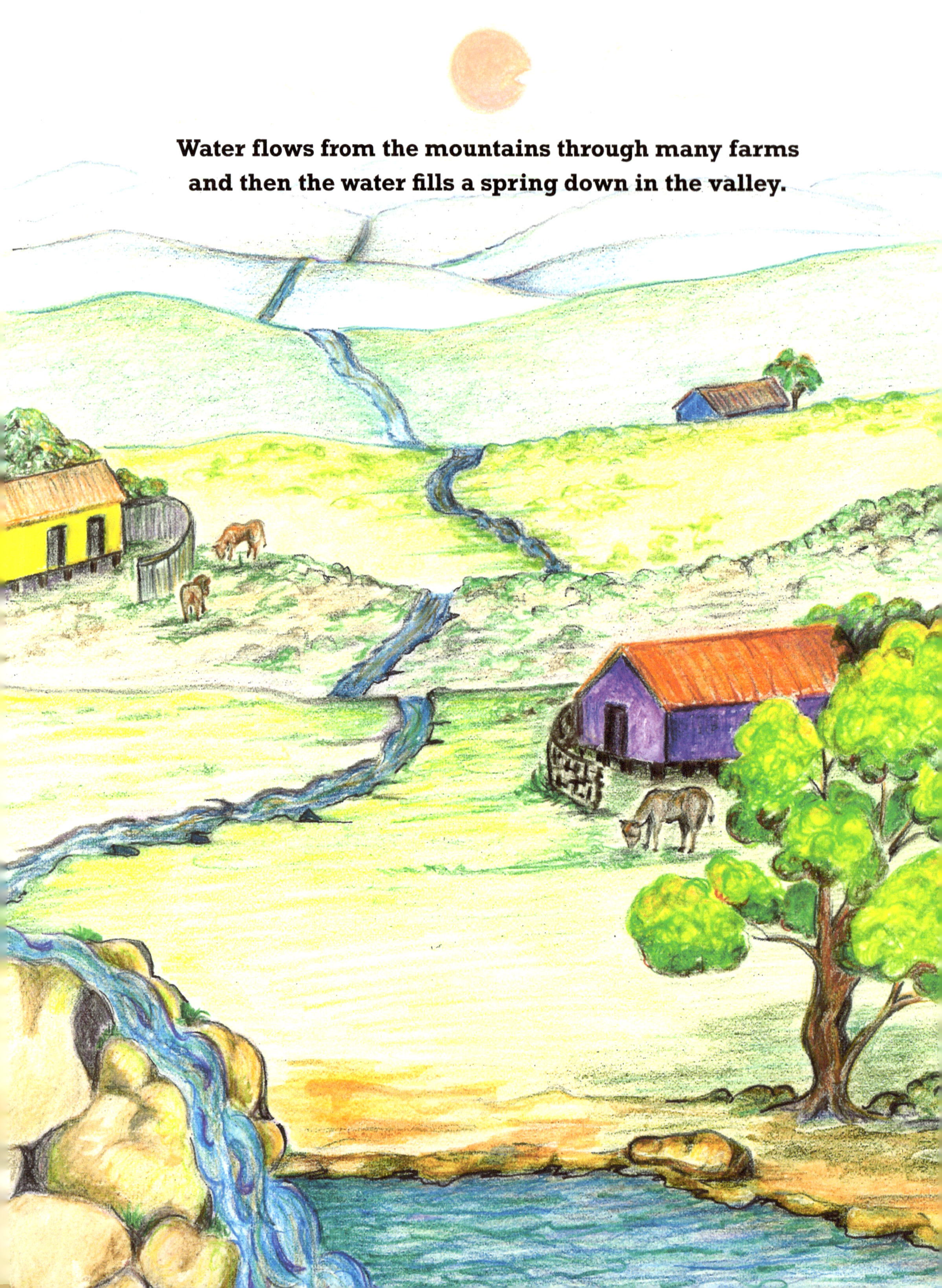

Water flows from the mountains through many farms and then the water fills a spring down in the valley.

Karimi and Kaedo fill their water casks and then start the long walk home.

When Karimi returns home, Karui and Marate have completed grinding corn. "We are ready to cook breakfast," Karui says to her mother.

After breakfast, Karui gathers her books and hurries off to school.

By the time Karui arrives at school,
the teacher has already started the lesson.

Karui enters the classroom and looks around for her friend Kathomi. "Oh no, Kathomi's seat is empty. Where is she?" she quietly asks.

Kathomi is sitting quietly in the dispensary, wishing she were in school and that her tummy didn't hurt so much.

"Kathomi is sick today because she drank dirty water with germs," Sister Mukiri, the community nurse, tells her mother, Kaedo.

"We must do something to get clean water.
Too many children are getting sick."

When two friends arrive at a village shop, they find it closed. "There is a water meeting today, let's go there," they both agree.

MUCEMANIO RUI
WATER MEETING
TODAY!

Everyone comes to the meeting.
"We will bring water to our village,"
they all agree after listening and talking.

The village chief says, "I will make a plan for bringing clean water to the village."

Chief Njilu and the village elder, Karithi, are on their way to the Divisional Office.

"I hope that Divisional Officer Munene will like our plan," Chief Njilu says to Karithi.

"*Jambo,* Divisional Officer Munene," Chief Njilu says. "Jambo sana," replies the Divisional Officer.

"Divisional Officer Munene, our plan is to bring water to the village, and we need your help," Chief Njilu continues.

"This is a good plan, Chief Njilu. I will speak to the Development Officer, and we will provide pipes," the Officer replies.

"We must decide on the route," the villagers agree as they start on the plan to bring clean water.

"We must try not to cut any trees."
"It is very good that we have the pipes," the villagers say as they dig a trench to hold the water pipes.

After much hard work, they place the water pipes in the trench.

“At last,” Karimi sighs, “I can drink clean water from a tap.”

As government officials arrive for the party,
Karui enjoys a glass of clean water.

Food is prepared for the party to celebrate the coming of clean water.

Friends arrive to celebrate and share their happiness over the new drinking water standpipe. Two women exchange greetings: Mama Kaario says, "Hujambo," and Mama Akou responds, "Sijambo."

Everyone is happy. Their hard work has brought clean water to the school and the village.

Now it is sunrise at Karui's house and everyone is asleep. Karimi, who no longer has to make the long walk to fetch water, sleeps especially soundly.

Mount Kenya, the highest peak in the country at
5,199 meters (17,058 feet) above sea level.

Lodwar
Moyale
Marsabit
Wajir
Eldoret
MOUNT
KENYA
Meru
KISUMU
Garissa
Nakuru
NAIROBI
Machakos
Lamu
Malindi
INDIAN
OCEAN
Mombasa

KENYA

Facts about Kenya and Meru County

Kenya is a large country on the east coast of Africa. It covers an area of 582,646 square kilometers (225,000 square miles), approximately the size of France. More than 80% of Kenyans in 2018, 51 million, live in the rural areas. In contrast, the majority of approximately 62 million people in France live in urban areas.[1-2]

Under the 2010 constitution, Kenya has a national government with three independent branches: the Legislative, the Executive, and the Judiciary. The constitution also created 47 counties, which have their own assemblies and executives headed by governors.[3] Kenya's diverse ecosystems include low coastal plains on the Indian Ocean, the Great Rift Valley, which runs from the North to the South, and the savanna grasslands bounded by escarpments and plateaus at the center. The grasslands are home to many wild animals such as rhinoceros, elephants and giraffes.

Children admiring a giraffe at the Giraffe Center in Langata, about ten kilometers (six miles) from the center of Nairobi, Kenya's capital. The Giraffe Center is a home for the endangered Rothschild giraffe, found only in the grasslands of East Africa.

The highest peak in the country is Mount Kenya at 5,199 meters (17,058 feet) above sea level. It is situated 16 kilometers (10 miles) from the Equator. Although near the Equator, Mount Kenya is always covered with snow. The summit of Mount Kenya is a twin pair of snow- covered rocky peaks called Batian and Nelion.[4]

Mount Kenya plays an important role in the lives of all Kenyans, but it is most significant for those living in surrounding counties. The four main ethnic groups living around Mount Kenya are Amerus (also called Meru), Gĩkũyũ, Embu, and Maasai.

The black and white colobus monkey is often found in forests around Mount Kenya. Colobus monkeys make long leaps between trees. Cutting of trees reduces water and endangers these monkeys.

The Amerus live east and north of Mount Kenya. The Amerus' name for Mount Kenya is Kirimara, meaning, "the one with white substance"–in other words, "snow." Traditionally, Mount Kenya is considered a sacred place where Murungu (Ngai), the Supreme Creator, resides. The Gîkûyû, Embu, and Maasai people also have names for Mount Kenya and all consider the mountain to be sacred. The name Kenya is derived from Kirinyaga or Kerenyaga, a Gîkûyû name meaning literally a place "that has ostriches." God's name in Gîkûyû is Mwene Nyaga, meaning "owner of the ostriches."[5]

Amerus are commonly called Meru, and the name also refers to the place occupied by Amerus and to their language. But the proper name for Meru language is Kimîîru, which varies slightly by geographic location within the county. The Meru people have a well-respected traditional form of governance and a legal system based on village councils (ciama) and a supreme council of elders (Njuri Ncheke) formed by elder houses (Nyumba ya Njuri). Njuri decisions are recognized by the modern Kenyan judicial system. The Merus have a high regard for individuals at various stages in life, and elders (senior citizens, also called village elders) are highly respected.[6]

Njuri Ncheke Council of Elders Headquarters located about nine kilometers (five and a half miles) north of Meru Town on Meru Maua Road. Trees are highly valued by Njuri Ncheke and usually Njuri Ncheke courthouses are located in forested areas.

The majority of Amerus and other ethnic groups in Kenya celebrate as a community to mark important events such as the birth of a child, completion of a new school or hospital, or—as in this story—the arrival of water in the village. Food served in village celebrations includes irio (beans mixed with vegetables) served with nyama choma (roast goat or beef). Another staple food in Meru is ugali, cornmeal porridge. It is served in a large bowl and usually eaten as a side dish with vegetable stew or any other food with sauce or gravy. To drink, porridge made from ground corn or millet was served in the old days; this has been replaced by tea. Tea is usually made with water boiled with milk and is served hot. Bananas and oranges are given to children during celebrations.

References

1. Kenya Population 2018. Accessed on November 23, 2018 at: World Population Review.com
2. The Statista: Urbanization in France 2017. Accessed on November 23, 2018 at: https://www.statista.com/statistics/270340/urbanization- in-france
3. The Council of Governors (CoG). The 47 Counties. Accessed on November 23, 2018 at: http://cog.go.ke/the-47-counties
4. The Geographical Association. Images of Kenya - A view of Mount Kenya. Accessed on November 23, 2018 at: https://www.geography.org.uk/Images-of- Kenya--A-view-of-Mount-Kenya
5. Wikipedia. Mt Kenya: Local culture. Accessed on May 19,2019 at: http://en.wikipedia.org/wiki/Mount_Kenya.
6. National Museum of Kenya. Meru: Historical background. Accessed on November 23, 2018 at: http://www.museums.or.ke/content/blogcategory/23/29/.

Water and Health

Water is vital to a healthy and productive life. Unfortunately, three in ten people around the world lack access to safely managed water services and six in ten lack adequate sanitation.[1]

The United Nations' 2030 Agenda for Sustainable Development recognizes safe drinking water, sanitation and good hygiene as vital for heathy communities.

Sustainable healthy communities should have what the World Heath Organizations calls, "safely managed" drinking water services– meaning drinking water at home that is free from contamination and available when needed."[2] To prevent spread of diseases, sustainable communities should also have access to safely managed sanitation services. This means that each household has its own means for excreta disposal on site or collected to an effective wastewater treatment system.

Two-thirds of Kenya is semi-arid or arid. The United Nations Children's Fund estimated that in 2015 seven out of 10 Kenyans used safely managed water supply while two out of five used safely managed sanitation services.[3]

Women at Mwirongudu water kiosk. Because water pressure is low, it takes several minutes to fill containers. This kiosk is part of the Tuuru Water Project.

However, the majority of people in rural areas lack access to water in their homes. They walk one kilometer or more (over half a mile) one or more times a day to collect water in containers of varying sizes. Children carry small gourds of approximately 2 liters (half a gallon) and their mothers carry about 20 liters (5 gallons) on their backs.

Families without ready access to clean water spend a large part of their time collecting water from sources far from home. Women in water-scarce areas may walk 8 kilometers or more (roughly five miles) for water, spending the first one to three hours of daylight on this chore. In some cases, young children—especially girls—carry water at the expense of attending school.

Rainfall is an important source of water for drinking and recharging lakes, rivers and underground water sources. During periods of prolonged drought, water shortages are severe in arid and semi-arid areas.

In Meru County, most days of the year are sunny and dry. However, there are two periods of the year when, semi- predictably, it may rain: 1) Intermittent "short rains" usually occur between October and December; 2) Heavier "long rains" usually occur between March and June. In the Highlands of Meru (altitude of 1,800 to 2,400 meters), the annual rainfall is over 1,000 millimeters per year and the weather is generally cool with an average temperature of about 200 C (68°F.)

The arid and semi-arid low-lying areas have much less rainfall and an average temperature of about 330 C (91°F.)

Many rivers originate from eastern slopes of Mount Kenya and flow through the rich agricultural areas of the Meru County to the Tana River. The rivers originating from the eastern slopes include Kathita, Thuci, and Ruguti. The Thantu and the Thangatha Rivers flow from the southern parts of the Nyambene Range to the Tana River.[4]

Changes in land use around the mountain, deforestation due to logging and land clearance, and the gradual melting of the mountain's glaciers are contributing to a reduction in the volume of the streams and rivers flowing down from the slopes of Mount Kenya.

References

1. United Nations. The Sustainable Development Agenda. Goal 6: Ensure access to water and sanitation for all. Accessed November 23, 2018 at: https://www. un.org/sustainabledevelopment/development-agenda/
2. World Health Organization. Progress on Drinking Water, Sanitation andHygiene. Accessed November 23, 2018 at: http://www.who.int/water_sanitation_health/publications/jmp-2017/en/
3. United Nations Children's Fund. Kenya: Statistics. Accessed November 23,2018 at: https://data.unicef.org/topic/water-and-sanitation/sanitation
4. Wangari E. Ameru. New York: The Rosen Publishing Group, Inc., 1995.

Children playing at Nkoronene Primary School. Notice the water harvesting tanks in the far background.

Reticulated giraffes crossing a road in Laikipia plateau, northeastern Kenya. This book is illustrated with giraffe characters because these beautiful animals can live in harsh environments with limited water.

www.ingramcontent.com/pod-product-compliance
Lightning Source LLC
LaVergne TN
LVHW070157110826
845147LV00002B/427

9780578520322